# YOUR KNOWLEDGE HAS VALUE

- We will publish your bachelor's and master's thesis, essays and papers

- Your own eBook and book - sold worldwide in all relevant shops

- Earn money with each sale

Upload your text at www.GRIN.com and publish for free

**Lena Meyer**

# Education, Science and Research in Medieval England

GRIN Publishing

**Bibliographic information published by the German National Library:**

The German National Library lists this publication in the National Bibliography; detailed bibliographic data are available on the Internet at http://dnb.dnb.de .

**Imprint:**

Copyright © 2014 GRIN Verlag GmbH
Print and binding: Books on Demand GmbH, Norderstedt Germany
ISBN: 978-3-656-95850-5

**This book at GRIN:**

http://www.grin.com/en/e-book/299327/education-science-and-research-in-medieval-england

**GRIN - Your knowledge has value**

Since its foundation in 1998, GRIN has specialized in publishing academic texts by students, college teachers and other academics as e-book and printed book. The website www.grin.com is an ideal platform for presenting term papers, final papers, scientific essays, dissertations and specialist books.

**Visit us on the internet:**

http://www.grin.com/

http://www.facebook.com/grincom

http://www.twitter.com/grin_com

# Learning and Science in Medieval England

**Table of Contents**

# 1. Schools and Education

About 120 schools are known to have existed in England during the period between the Norman Conquest in 1066 and the Reformation in 1517 (Orme 1976: XI). However, such numbers must remain vague and can only offer limited insight into medieval English learning. This is partly due to the relatively low amount of source material, but also the wide range of highly differing institutions which were all referred to with the term "school" (c.f. ibid.: 2f). Still, some distinctions can be made and similarities can be found in almost all medieval English schools, mostly involving the curricula, manners of education and the people teaching at and attending schools. Additionally, academic institutions had a high social impact on their respective surroundings (c.f. ibid.: 32f).

## 1.1 Types of schools

As mentioned above, the detection of distinct school-forms is rather difficult. Orme categorized these various institutions in three major types: secular schools, private secular schools and schools of religious orders (c.f. ibid.: 1f).

Secular schools were open to the public and there were almost no restrictions that limited the admission to one of those schools, except for sex (only males were allowed to attend school), fees and dispensability from any other work (c.f. ibid.: 1). The restriction of fees lessened during the course of the $14^{th}$ century, when some wealthy benefactors (usually bishops, merchants, members of the nobility etc.) endowed schools with money and/or property, thereby allowing the respective masters to teach for free (c.f. ibid.). The masters of such schools were secular priests, clerks and laymen, but (unlike monks and friars) usually not members of a religious order – and so were their scholars (c.f. ibid.).

Private secular schools were insofar more restricted, as they were located in large monasteries that only few sons of wealthy magnates were able to attend (c.f. ibid.). As Orme states, such schools did not necessarily provide a higher quality of education, but involved much fewer pupils (c.f. ibid.). The masters of private schools were mostly secular teachers, but also members of the clergy, though apparently never monks (c.f. ibid.).

Schools of religious orders had the defined aim of educating future members of their respective orders and therefore, unlike any other school-form, provided a more or less clear-cut future for their scholars. Such schools were rather enclosed, small and private and only intended for religious purposes; monks and friars worked as masters and instructed their pupils with the specific knowledge needed in order to lead a monastic life and to work and behave accordingly (c.f. ibid.: 1f).

## 1.2 The Curriculum

According to Orme, the typical curriculum of a medieval English school was made up of three major parts: reading and singing, grammar and literary studies and optional higher studies (c.f. ibid.: 2f). When comparing the curricula of medieval and modern times, similarities as well as differences can be recognized: while both function comparable to steps that each student has to climb in order to access further and more defined knowledge, medieval education put a higher emphasis on religion and learning by heart as a manner of pedagogy.

Reading and singing covered learning the Alphabet, pronunciation and chanting, thereby helping students remember the correct pronunciation of words and biblical verses and also preparing them for a rather likely clerical career (c.f. ibid.). This first stage formed the basis of any further education and was mainly intended for children (c.f. ibid.). Grammar and literary studies were the next stage of learning and involved reading prose and poems, but also studying literary texts and achieving experience with literary criticism (c.f. ibid.). This manner of reading and examining texts might be slightly comparable to its modern equivalent. Higher education was only accessible for those students who had a thorough understanding of Latin and the money required to be educated even further (c.f. ibid.). The offered courses were concerned with arts, medicine, law and theology which Orme regards as the "third and highest grade of medieval education" (ibid.: 2).

As schools were mainly led by only one master (and, in some cases, an assistant), it was impossible to cover each and every aspect of a curriculum as broad as that of medieval England in one school (c.f. ibid. 2f). Thus, different schools were concerned with different aspects of the curriculum and therefore had different main focuses which complicates the detection of distinct schools even further (c.f. ibid.). Another problem already mentioned beforehand is the source material itself which does not clearly distinguish between schools of any kind – be they schools of song or grammar, public, clerical or private (c.f. ibid.).

4

## 1.3 Distinguishing schools

Still, some distinctions can be made, for example those between elementary schools and universities, the first emerging only at the end of the Middle Ages when some schools explicitly excluded their teachings from basic subjects and focused on advanced students only (c.f. ibid.: 3f). This development propelled the emergence of universities, even though such institutions did not exist until the 13th century and even then, the boundaries between the education offered at schools and the studies taught at universities remained blurred (c.f. ibid.).

Some examples might illustrate this: scholars could attend grammar schools and further develop their knowledge at universities, but they could also learn basic grammar at some universities; there were art schools, even though the universities had the self-conception of being the centers of art-studies; when learning basic grammar at schools, students also encountered theories of logic which was actually a subject taught at universities only (c.f. ibid.). Once again, any finer distinction is difficult and confusing, as the obscured boundaries between the various school-forms "had [their] verbal equivalent since the universities were generally known as 'the schools' [...] and their undergraduates as 'scholars'. You 'went to school' at Oxford and attended 'the schools' or lecture rooms of the masters there" (ibid.). Still, only a rather small amount of students ever finished their academic career, the majority of them leaving without a degree (c.f. Grant 1996: 38).

Still, universities and their educational system bear a striking similarity to those of modern days, especially regarding their concept of the studies of arts (c.f. ibid.: 50f). While the students of theology, law and medicine were aiming for a later profession in these respective fields, students of arts were learning for the sole purpose of learning (c.f. ibid.). Grant states that, even though such studies did not serve society directly or in a mere practical way, they nevertheless were the basis for modern scientific research and enabled its development in the first place (c.f. ibid.).

**1.4 A usual school day**

The definition of a typical day at an English school during the Middle Ages appears to be as difficult and obscured as that of schools in general. Again, there are some aspects that seem to repeat themselves, thereby allowing at least an approximate image: according to Orme, there were only male students and masters, the former starting their studies at the age of seven, but there were also older pupils up till the age of 20 (c.f. Orme: 20). Regarding the latter, it remains unclear what requirements a master had to exhibit in order to be allowed to teach; presumably, being a cleric was not among these (expect for schools of religious orders), neither was being a graduate (c.f. ibid.: 19). In fact,

> Teaching was a traditional resort of clerks whom martial entanglements had barred from the priesthood [and the] basic requirements in a medieval schoolmaster were simple: sufficient knowledge of grammar and an honest reputation (ibid.).

When reconstructing a usual school day, a raw assembly of reoccurring elements can be made out: a relatively small group of young men gathered in one large room, bowing their tonsured heads at their master and having a seat in one of the benches (c.f. ibid.). Their day started at six o'clock in the morning and ended 12 hours later, only disrupted by short breaks for eating (c.f. ibid.). There were holidays, however, they had religious purposes and were therefore dedicated to prayer, not necessarily leisure (c.f. ibid.).

The language most commonly used in the classroom appears to be Latin; still, the younger students were taught in French first, before moving on to the language most of them would use in their later professions (c.f. ibid.: 22). After the 14th century, pupils were also taught in English, but Latin always remained an important scholarly language (c.f. ibid.).

**1.5 Schools and Education – a conclusion**

Even though their exact form is hard to define, it can be stated that schools first emerged as centers of education and knowledge in England during the 12th century (c.f. ibid.: 1). They were mostly urban, but, over the course of their development, smaller schools were also established in villages (c.f. ibid.: 32). These institutions served their respective communities by educating the local children, but larger schools were also attended by students from other regions (c.f. ibid.: 32f). Schools as well as universities depended on political and financial support, provided by a stable regional society and wealthy benefactors (c.f. ibid.: 1f, 32f).

## 2. Science and Research

Grant pleads against the underestimation of medieval scientific knowledge by stating that, "contrary to prevailing opinion, the roots of modern science were planted in the ancient and medieval world long before the Scientific Revolution" (Grant: I). Similar to detecting distinct school-forms, the respective fields of medieval science are hard to define; there was medical as well as artistic and literary knowledge and science did not necessarily involve a strict reading of the Bible (c.f. ibid.: 33f, 22). Interestingly enough, English was not as commonly used in scientific contexts as it is today – the language of science was Latin and therefore its most important basis (c.f. Taavitsainen a. Pahta 2004: XV). Many ancient manuscripts were not only rediscovered, but also translated and adapted, providing medieval scholars with thought-provoking impulse (c.f. Horobin a. Smith 2002: 167). Still, most of these sources were heavily fragmented and religious schools and monasteries remained the rather enclosed centers of knowledge (c.f. ibid. & Grant: 22).

### 2.1 Scientific Sources and Topics

During the 12$^{th}$ century, a rising number of texts of Greek and Arabic origin was rediscovered and translated, paving the way for future discoveries and propelling the emergence of science as it is known today (c.f. Taavitsainen a. Pahta: XV & Grant: I, 22f). Due to the increasing development of universities which further supported the exchange of knowledge, nourished its intercultural flow and formed scientific communities such as Oxford and Cambridge, nearly all important sources were available in Latin during the 13$^{th}$ century (c.f. Grant: 33f). These included works by Euclid, Ptolemy and Archimedes, but also Aristotle whose philosophy became an important aspect of medieval science in many of its fields (c.f. ibid.: 26f).

Regarding the topics that medieval scientists dealt with, again a problem of exact and terms and definitions arises: "[T]he conception of what counts as science and scientific writing has undergone fundamental changes in the course of time. [...] Distinctions between various branches of science were not made in the present way [...]" (Taavitsainen a. Pahta: 1). There appears to have been a strong belief in the power of the cosmos and its influence on daily life, including for example sickness, nature, medicine, but also the correct timing of acts of worship and agriculture (c.f. ibid.: 1f). Astronomy and astrology were therefore believed to offer insights into all matters of daily life, as the huge cosmos of the planets could be transferred to the smaller one of mankind (c.f. ibid.).

## 2.2 Scientific Writing

Even though definite parameters of what the Middle Ages considered scientific writing are hard to detect, present-day scientific writing appears to be highly influenced by these earlier stages (c.f. ibid.: XV, 1f). This assumption can be made on the basis of the nearly complete continuity from its most early stages (the Anglo-Saxon period, dating from 550-1066) to more recent ones and from then onwards till today (c.f. ibid.: XV). However, the style of these treatises underwent many changes, including the notion of what is to be regarded as scientific in the first place, thereby obscuring the distinct stages of its course; still, a development from a rather detached style of writing to a more involved one and back again can be found (c.f. ibid.). Surprisingly, there appears to be continuity regarding scientific consensus and the manner of approaching questions: just like modern researchers, medieval scientists considered one problem from many angles and many authors composed solutions for the same question and even though there seems to have been an overall consensus, details remained debated (c.f. Grant: 159f). Yet, there is also a shift in scientific language and vocabulary: while earlier texts mostly use elaborate Latin, which was the language of the educated clergy who were usually the ones writing and studying scientific papers, later texts tend to be written in often vernacularized forms of English (c.f. Taavitsainen a. Pahta: XV, 8f).

Regardless of the changes in style and topics, there are many similarities which medieval scientific writing still shares with that of more recent publication; the most striking one might be its self-referential system, examining earlier works and criticizing their authors (c.f. ibid.: 1f). Scientific works were also fairly open to ideas from other regions and often, especially in their earlier stages, expressed such ideas in technical terms borrowed from another language (c.f. ibid.: 2f, 74f). This led to "polyglot discourse communities" (ibid.: 74) comparable to those of today, but also complicates the translation of such works (c.f. Horobin a. Smith: 167).

## 2.3 Science versus Religion

The relation of science and religion and their respective effects upon one another are hard to define – a problem of terms arises, comparable to that of schools and education as illustrated above: it remains unclear, what the Middle Ages regarded as scientific writing (c.f. ibid.: 1). Furthermore, the course of its development appears to be almost as obscure as that of the medieval educational system. Taavitsainen and Pahta propose a theory stating that medieval scientific writing had a rather strict focus on religious aspects (c.f. Taavitsainen a. Pahta: 3f), while Grant offers a more diversified view (c.f. Grant: 1-14).

There appear to be some definite aspects, as Grant suggests (c.f. Grant: 1-14). While the Christian belief-system was regarded as universal truth, the secular Greek and Arabic influences were met with disaffirmation due to their vagueness and constant re-evaluation of questions and problems (c.f. ibid.: 2f). Yet, at the end of the $2^{nd}$ century, Christian academics began to include foreign ideas into their theological studies: such influences were not regarded as mere good or bad anymore, but their value depended on their usage (c.f. ibid.). Even though philosophy and science with Greek origin were still regarded pagan, they "could be studied as 'handmaidens of theology'" (ibid.: 3), aiding understanding of the Bible by offering a basis for the higher studies theology and scripture (c.f. ibid. 3f). This can be seen as a compromise, avoiding both complete inclusion and neglect of new ideas; it is important to bear in mind, however, that medieval academics did not include these thoughts in order to gain knowledge and broaden their scientific horizon, but rather to help them find better approaches to the Bible and its content (c.f. ibid.: 5).

## 2.4 Science and Medicine, Science and Nature

Unlike scientific texts covering religious or philosophical topics, medical writing seemingly tended toward a broader readership, as Taavitsainen and Pahta indicate by stating that much of the written medieval medical knowledge was vernacularized (c.f. ibid.: 2). Cockayne subscribes to their theories in his studies of the so called Leech Books and similarly concludes that England's early inhabitants already knew how to find healthy and healing food and other means of therapy in the nature that surrounded them – and also documented such findings (c.f. Cockayne 1865: VIIf). Even though Latin was the most important language of science and learning, these texts covering common and practical issues were already available in a vernacularized English form (c.f. ibid.: XXIII & Taavitsainen a. Pahta: 8f). This propelled a later development, namely the vernacularisation of other scientific topics, but also practical ones such as cookery or literary ones such as poetry (c.f. ibid.: 11). The rediscovery of Greek and Arabic texts, as mentioned above, immensely affected medical writing, as many of the later medical treatises were adapted from and inspired by such sources (c.f. Taavitsainen a. Pahta: 2). Due to Arabic tradition, medical approaches linked back to philosophical ones, thereby also influencing other fields of medieval science (c.f. ibid.).

The so called natural philosophy, stemming from a Greek body of thought and hugely influenced by Aristotle, had its roots in such foreign influences as well (c.f. Grant: 135f, 158f). Even though this scientific branch is similar to the modern field of biology, there are significant differences: while modern biologists support their theses with empiric data and experiments, medieval scientists based their research on mere though-experiments (c.f. ibid.: 153f, 159). A reason for this can not only be found in a lack of equipment, but also in the original idea of natural philosophy itself, in which Aristotle suggested that all bodies and substances are harmonically intertwined with their respective surroundings and that practical experiments would change this state (c.f. ibid. 159f). A scientist studying natural philosophy should therefore observe and find explanations for these harmonic conditions instead of disrupting them (c.f. ibid.).

## 2.5 Science and Research – a conclusion

Even though the Middle Ages are often portrayed as an unprogressive period of history, lacking scientific knowledge and viewing the Bible as only true explanation for the world, they presumably formed the basis of what is known as science today (c.f. ibid.: I). While there are differences as well as similarities when compared to its modern equivalent, medieval science emerged from a mixture of traditions, belief-systems and societies (c.f. Taavitsainen a. Pahta: 2 & Grant: I, 2f, 18-33). This was only possible via translations and organization of foreign treatises, leading to a special style of writing – a style which at first favored the academic language Latin, but rather quickly induced the production of scientific texts written in vernacular variants of English as well (c.f. Taavitsainen a. Pahta: XV, 8f). A new concept of knowledge arose, allowing the individual to study for the sole purpose of studying and thereby stimulating the emergence of research, scientific discussions and further exchange of thoughts (c.f. Grant: 49f, 159f). Still, one of the most important goals of medieval science, if not its foremost ambition was even better understanding of the Bible and its teachings; nevertheless, these efforts paved the way for the ages of Renaissance and the Scientific Revolution (c.f. Grant: I, 5, 10f, 168f).

# Bibliography

- Cockayne, O. (Ed.), *Leechdoms, Wortcunning and Starcraft of Early England*, 2, London, 1865.

- Grant, E., The Foundations of Modern Science in the Middle Ages. Their Religious, Institutional, and Intellectual Contexts, Cambridge University, 1996.

- Herdan, G., Chaucer's Authorship of The Equatorie of the Planetis. The Use of Romance Vocabulary as Evidence, in: *Language,* 32 (2), 1956, p. 254-259.

- Horobin, S. a. Smith, J., An Introduction to Middle English, Oxford University, 2002, p. 167-169.

- Orme, N., Education in the West of England 1066-1548, University of Exeter, 1976.

- Taavitsainen, I. a. Pahta, P. (Ed.), *Medical and Scientific Writing in Late Medieval English*, Cambridge University, 2004.